Basic Sleepy-Time Friend

Skill Level

■■□□ EASY

Finished Measurement

18 inches tall

Materials

- Red Heart Super Saver medium (worsted) weight acrylic yarn (solids: 7 oz/364 yds/198g per skein; heathers: 5 oz/236 yds/141g per skein): See yarn requirements for each individual animal
- Size H/8/5mm crochet hook or size needed to obtain gauge
- 10-inch round pillow or fiberfill
- Stitch markers: 8
- Tapestry needle

Gauge

Rnds 1–4 of face = 2¼ inches

Pattern Notes

Weave in loose ends as work progresses.

Join or attach designated colors with slip stitch as indicated unless otherwise stated.

Chain-3 at beginning of row counts as first double crochet unless otherwise stated.

Mark right sides of work (RS) with stitch markers.

Face and back of head are worked in the round without turning at the ends of rounds.

Use and change yarn colors according to directions for each individual animal.

Use a body color for sewing on tails and tummies so that stitches aren't visible on the flip side.

Basic Friend

Face

Rnd 1 (RS): With designated color, ch 2, work 6 sc in first ch, **join** (see Pattern Notes) in first sc. (6 sc)

Rnd 2: Ch 1, work 2 sc in each sc around. Join in first sc. (12 sc)

Rnd 3: Ch 1, 2 sc in same st, sc in next st, *2 sc in next st, sc in next st, rep from * around. Join in first sc. (18 sc)

Rnd 4: Ch 1, 2 sc in same st, sc in next 2 sts, *2 sc in next st, sc in next 2 sts, rep from * around. Join in first sc. (24 sc)

Rnd 5: Ch 1, 2 sc in same st, sc in next 3 sts, *2 sc in next st, sc in next 3 sts, rep from * around. Join in first sc. (30 sc)

Rnd 6: Ch 1, sc in same st, sc in next 2 sts, *2 sc in next st, sc in next 4 sts, rep from * around, end with 2 sc in next st, sc in last st. Join in first sc. (36 sc)

Rnd 7: Ch 1, sc in same st, sc in next st, *2 sc in next st, sc in next 5 sts, rep from * around, end with 2 sc in next st, sc in last 3 sts. Join in first sc. (42 sc)

Rnd 8: Ch 1, sc in same st, sc in next 4 sts, *2 sc in next st, sc in next 6 sts, rep from * around, end with 2 sc in next st, sc in last st. Join in first sc. (48 sc)

Rnd 9: Ch 1, sc in same st, sc in next st, *2 sc in next st, sc in next 7 sts, rep from * around, end with 2 sc in next st, sc in last 5 sts. Join in first sc. (54 sc)

Rnd 10: Ch 1, 2 sc in same st, sc in next 8 sts, *2 sc in next st, sc in next 8 sts, rep from * around. Join in first sc. *(60 sc)*

Rnd 11: Ch 1, sc in same st, sc in next 5 sts, *2 sc in next st, sc in next 9 sts, rep from * around, end with 2 sc in next st, sc in last 3 sts. Join in first sc. *(66 sc)*

Rnd 12: Ch 1, 2 sc in same st, *sc in next 16 sts, 2 sc in next st, rep from * around, end with sc in last 14 sts. Join in first sc, fasten off face color. *(70 sc)*

Rnd 13: Attach designated color in same st, ch 1, sc in same st, sc in next 3 sts, *2 sc in next st, sc in next 17 sts, rep from * around, end with 2 sc in next st, sc in last 11 sts. Join in first sc. *(74 sc)*

Rnds 14–17: Ch 1, sc in same st, sc in each st around. Join in first sc. At end of rnd 17, fasten off. *(74 sc)*

Back of Head
Work rnds 1–17 of face using designated color(s).

Body
Row 1 (RS): With designated color, ch 24, dc in 4th ch from hook *(first 3 chs count as first dc)*, dc in each ch across, turn. *(22 dc)*

Row 2: Ch 3 *(see Pattern Notes)*, dc in next 3 sts, (2 dc in next st, dc in next 5 sts) 3 times, turn. *(25 dc)*

Row 3: Ch 3, dc in next 6 sts, (2 dc in next st, dc in next 8 sts) 2 times, turn. *(27 dc)*

Row 4: Ch 3, dc in next 5 sts, (2 dc in next st, dc in next 6 sts) 3 times, turn. *(30 dc)*

Row 5: Ch 3, dc in next 9 sts, (2 dc in next st, dc in next 9 sts) 2 times, turn. *(32 dc)*

First Arm
Row 1 (WS): Ch 3, dc in next 5 sts, turn. *(6 dc)*

Row 2: Ch 3, dc in next 5 sts. Fasten off, turn.

Row 3: Attach designated color in first st, ch 3, dc in next st, **dc dec** *(see Stitch Guide)* over next 2 sts, dc in last 2 sts, turn. *(5 dc)*

Row 4: Ch 3, (dc dec over next 2 sts) 2 times. Fasten off, turn. *(3 dc)*

Continue Body
Row 6 (WS): Along row 5 of body, sk the 6 sts at the base of the first arm, sk 1 more st, attach designated color in next st, ch 3, dc in next 5 sts, (2 dc in next st, dc in next 5 sts) 2 times. Leave rem 7 sts unworked, turn. *(20 dc)*

Row 7: Ch 3, dc in next 5 sts, (2 dc in next st, dc in next 6 sts) 2 times, turn. *(22 dc)*

Row 8: Ch 3, dc in each st across, turn.

Row 9: Ch 3, dc in next 9 sts, 2 dc in next st, dc in last 11 sts, turn. *(23 dc)*

First Leg
Row 1 (WS): Ch 3, dc in next 9 sts of the body, turn. Leave rem sts unworked. *(10 dc)*

Row 2: Ch 3, dc dec over next 2 sts, dc in last 7 sts, turn. *(9 dc)*

Row 3: Ch 3, dc in next 6 sts, dc dec over last 2 sts, turn. *(8 dc)*

Row 4: Ch 3, dc dec over next 2 sts, dc in last 5 sts. Fasten off, turn. *(7 dc)*

Row 5: Attach designated color in first dc, ch 3, dc in next 2 sts, dc dec over next 2 sts, dc in last 2 sts, turn. *(6 dc)*

Row 6: Ch 3, (dc dec over next 2 sts) 2 times, dc in last st. Fasten off, turn. *(4 dc)*

2nd Leg
Row 1 (WS): Along row 9 of body, sk the 10 sts at the base of the first leg, sk the next 3 sts, attach designated color in next st, ch 3, dc in next 9 sts, turn. *(10 dc)*

Row 2: Ch 3, dc in next 7 sts, dc dec over next 2 sts, turn. *(9 dc)*

Row 3: Ch 3, dc dec over next 2 sts, dc in last 6 sts, turn. *(8 dc)*

Row 4: Ch 3, dc in next 5 sts, dc dec over last 2 sts. Fasten off, turn. *(7 dc)*

Row 5: Attach designated color in first dc, ch 3, dc in next st, dc dec over next 2 sts, dc in last 3 sts, turn. *(6 dc)*

Row 6: Ch 3, (dc dec over next 2 sts) 2 times, dc in last st. Fasten off, turn. *(4 dc)*

2nd Arm

Row 1 (WS): Along the rem sts of row 5 of the body, sk first free st. Attach designated color in next st, ch 3, dc in last 5 sts, turn. *(6 dc)*

Row 2: Ch 3, dc in next 5 sts. Fasten off, turn.

Row 3: Attach designated color in first st, ch 3, dc in next st, dc dec over next 2 sts, dc in last 2 sts, turn. *(5 dc)*

Row 4: Ch 3, (dc dec over next 2 sts) 2 times. Fasten off. *(3 dc)*

Tummy

With designated color, work first 6 rnds of face. Fasten off. *(36 sc)*

Optional Bow

Row 1: With desired color, ch 13, sc in 2nd ch from hook and in each ch across, turn. *(12 sc)*

Rows 2–8: Working in **back lps** *(see Stitch Guide)* only, ch 1, sc in each st across, turn. *(12 sc)* At end of row 8 (RS), fasten off, turn.

Bow Band

Row 1: Work through both lps, sk first 5 sts, reattach yarn in next st, ch 1, sc in same st, sc in next st, turn, leaving rem sts unworked. *(2 sc)*

Rows 2–6: Ch 1, sc in each st across, turn. At end of row 6, leaving 10-inch tail to finish bow, fasten off.

Ear & Tail

Ear and tail patterns vary and will be found in each individual animal's section.

Assembly

Lightly steam all pieces, shaping to smooth edges, if necessary. Fold face in half, use stitch markers to mark each end of folded edge. Refold face so stitch markers meet, and again use stitch markers to mark each end of folded edge. This divides face into quarters and will aid in placement of ears and features. Mark the back of head in same way, dividing it into quarters. Following individual face diagrams, use black to **backstitch, satin stitch or straight stitch** *(see illustrations)* as necesary to stitch mouth, nose and eyelids onto RS of face.

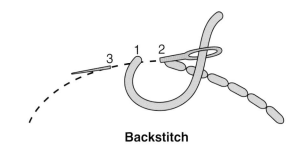

Backstitch

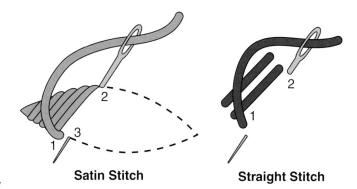

Satin Stitch   **Straight Stitch**

With RS up, sew ears to front of face in position individually designated, between rows 14 and 15.

With RS up, sew tummy to center of right side of body.

On WS of body, center and sew tail along row 7.

With WS tog, begin to sew back of head and face tog, matching quarter marks, and leaving face markers in place. Before closing, insert pillow or stuff with fiberfill, and continue sewing to enclose. Fold body piece together so that arms meet, use a stitch marker to mark center neck. With RS up, align neck marker with the face marker below smile. Pin neck edge in place along the seam line of head, measuring 3 inches to each side of neck center for placement of shoulder ends. Sew tog.

For optional bow, wrap the bow band across WS of bow, and back around RS until band row 6 meets band row 1. Use the 10-inch tail of yarn to stitch these rows tog to encase bow. Adjust bow shape as needed, and sew in desired position above an ear, or at the bottom of face near center neck. ●

Bear Friend

Skill Level

■■□□ EASY

Finished Measurement

18 inches tall

Materials

- Red Heart Super Saver medium (worsted) weight acrylic yarn (7 oz/364 yds/198g per skein):
    1 skein each #312 black and
        #336 warm brown
    10 yds #319 cherry red
- Size H/8/5mm crochet hook or size needed to obtain gauge
- 10-inch round pillow or fiberfill
- Stitch markers: 8
- Tapestry needle

Gauge

Rnds 1–4 of face = 2¼ inches

Pattern Note

Using directions and colors indicated, follow instructions for Basic Friend on page 1.

Bear Friend

Face

Rnds 1–12: With warm brown.

Rnds 13–17: With black.

Back of Head

Rnds 1–17: With black.

Body

Rows 1–5: With black.

First Arm

Rows 1 & 2: With black.

Rows 3 & 4: With warm brown.

Continue Body

Rows 6–9: With black.

First Leg

Rows 1–4: With black.

Rows 5 & 6: With warm brown.

2nd Leg

Rows 1–4: With black.

Rows 5 & 6: With warm brown.

2nd Arm
Rows 1 & 2: With black.

Rows 3 & 4: With warm brown.

Tummy
Rnds 1–6: With warm brown.

Ear
Make 2.

Rnd 1 (RS): With warm brown, ch 2, work 6 sc in first ch. Join in first sc. *(6 sc)*

Rnd 2: Ch 1, work 2 sc in each sc around. Join in first sc. *(12 sc)*

Rnd 3: Ch 1, 2 sc in same st, sc in next st, *2 sc in next st, sc in next st, rep from * around. Join in first sc, fasten off warm brown. *(18 sc)*

Next row: Now working in rows, attach black in first st of rnd 3, ch 1, sc in same st, (2 sc in next st, sc in next 2 sts) 5 times, turn, leaving rem sts unworked. *(21 sc)*

Final row: Ch 1, 2 sc in same st, (sc in next 3 sts, 2 sc in next st) 5 times. Fasten off. *(27 sc)*

Tail
Row 1: With black, ch 2, 3 sc in 2nd ch from hook, turn. *(3 sc)*

Row 2: Ch 1, 2 sc in same st, sc in next st, 2 sc in last st, turn. *(5 sc)*

Rows 3 & 4: Ch 1, sc in same st, sc in each st across, turn. *(5 sc)*

Row 5: Ch 1, **sc dec** *(see Stitch Guide)* over first 2 sts, sc in next st, sc dec over last 2 sts, turn. *(3 sc)*

Row 6: Ch 1, sc in same st, sc in each st across. Fasten off. *(3 sc)*

Bow
All rows: With cherry red.

Finishing
See Bear diagram for ear and facial feature placement. Assemble as for Basic Friend. ●

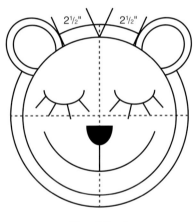

Bear Friend
Diagram

Bunny Friend

Skill Level

 EASY

Finished Measurement

18 inches tall

Materials

- Red Heart Super Saver medium (worsted) weight acrylic yarn (solids: 7 oz/364 yds/198g per skein; heathers: 5 oz/236 yds/141g per skein):
  - 1 skein each #326 oatmeal and #400 grey heather
  - 10 yds #373 petal pink
  - 5 yds each #312 black and #316 soft white
- Size H/8/5mm crochet hook or size needed to obtain gauge
- Tapestry needle
- 10-inch round pillow or fiberfill
- Stitch markers: 8

Gauge

Rnds 1–4 of face = 2¼ inches

Pattern Note

Using directions and colors indicated, follow instructions for Basic Friend on page 1.

Bunny Friend

Face

Rnds 1–12: With grey heather.

Rnds 13–17: With oatmeal.

Back of Head

Rnds 1–17: With oatmeal.

Body

Rows 1–5: With oatmeal.

First Arm

Rows 1 & 2: With oatmeal.

Rows 3 & 4: With grey heather.

Continue Body

Rows 6–9: With oatmeal.

First Leg

Rows 1–4: With oatmeal.

Rows 5 & 6: With grey heather.

2nd Leg

Rows 1–4: With oatmeal.

Rows 5 & 6: With grey heather.

2nd Arm

Rows 1 & 2: With oatmeal.

Rows 3 & 4: With grey heather.

Tummy

Rnds 1–6: With grey heather.

Ear

Make 2.

Row 1 (RS): With grey heather, ch 23, sc in 2nd ch from hook, sc in next 5 chs, hdc in next 6 chs, dc in next 9 chs, 7 dc in last ch. Now working along opposite side of beg ch, dc in next 9 chs, hdc in next 6 chs, sc in last 6 chs, turn. *(6 sc, 6 hdc, 25 dc, 6 hdc, 6 sc)*

Row 2 (RS): Ch 1, sc in same st, sc in next 3 sts, hdc in next 8 sts, dc in next 10 sts, (2 dc in next st) 5 times,

dc in next 10 sts, hdc in next 8 sts, sc in last 4 sts. Fasten off. *(4 sc, 8 hdc, 30 dc, 8 hdc, 4 sc)*

Tail

Rnds 1–3: With soft white, work rnds 1–3 of face. Fasten off.

Bow

All rows: With petal pink.

Finishing

See Bunny diagram for ear and facial feature placement. Assemble as for Basic Friend. ●

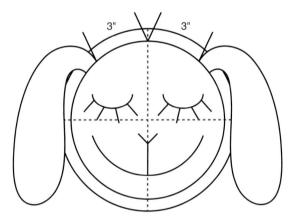

Bunny Friend
Diagram

Doggy Friend

Skill Level
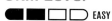 EASY

Finished Measurement
18 inches tall

Materials
- Red Heart Super Saver medium (worsted) weight acrylic yarn (7 oz/364 yds/198g per skein):
  - 1 skein each #365 coffee and #316 soft white
  - 10 yds #1102 freshmint
  - 5 yds #312 black
- Size H/8/5mm crochet hook or size needed to obtain gauge
- 10-inch round pillow or fiberfill
- Stitch markers: 8
- Tapestry needle

Gauge
Rnds 1–4 of face = 2¼ inches

Pattern Notes
Using directions and colors indicated, follow instructions for Basic Friend on page 1.

Chain-2 at beginning of row does not count as first stitch unless otherwise stated.

Doggy Friend

Face
Rnds 1–12: With soft white.

Rnds 13–17: With coffee.

Back of Head
Rnds 1–17: With coffee.

Body
Rows 1–5: With coffee.

First Arm
Rows 1 & 2: With coffee.

Rows 3 & 4: With soft white.

Continue Body
Rows 6–9: With coffee.

First Leg
Rows 1–4: With coffee.

Rows 5 & 6: With soft white.

2nd Leg
Rows 1–4: With coffee.

Rows 5 & 6: With soft white.

2nd Arm
Rows 1 & 2: With coffee.

Rows 3 & 4: With soft white.

Tummy
Rnds 1–6: With soft white.

Ear
Make 2.

Row 1 (RS): With coffee, ch 13, dc in 4th ch from hook, dc in next 8 chs, 7 dc in last ch. Now working along opposite side of beg ch, dc in next 10 chs, turn. *(27 dc)*

Row 2: Ch 1, sc in same st, sc in next 3 sts, hdc in next 3 sts, dc in next 2 sts, (2 dc in next st, dc in next st) 5 times, dc in next st, hdc in next 3 sts, sc in last 4 sts. Fasten off. *(4 sc, 3 hdc, 18 dc, 3 hdc, 4 sc)*

Tail
Row 1: With soft white, ch 2, sc in 2nd ch from hook, turn. *(1 sc)*

Row 2: Ch 1, 2 sc in same st, turn. *(2 sc)*

Row 3: Ch 1, sc in each st across. Fasten off soft white, turn. *(2 sc)*

Row 4: Join coffee in first st, **ch 2** *(see Pattern Notes)*, hdc in first st, sc in last st, turn. *(1 hdc, 1 sc)*

Row 5: Ch 1, sc in same st, sc in last st, turn. *(2 sc)*

Row 6: Ch 2, hdc in first st, sc in last st, turn. *(1 hdc, 1 sc)*

Rows 7–10: [Rep rows 5 and 6 consecutively] 2 times.

Rows 11–18: Ch 1, sc in same st, sc in last st, turn. At end of row 18, fasten off. *(2 sc)*

Bow
All rows: With freshmint.

Finishing
See Doggy diagram for ear and facial feature placement. Assemble as for Basic Friend. ●

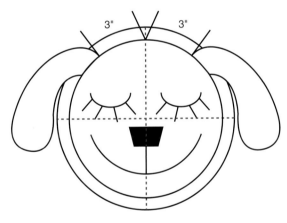

Doggy Friend
Diagram

Kitty Friend

Skill Level

 EASY

Finished Measurement

18 inches tall

Materials

- Red Heart Super Saver medium (worsted) weight acrylic yarn (7 oz/364 yds/198g per skein):
    1 skein each #235 lemon, #316 soft white and #321 gold
    5 yds #312 black
- Size H/8/5mm crochet hook or size needed to obtain gauge
- 10-inch round pillow or fiberfill
- Stitch markers: 8
- Tapestry needle

Gauge

Rnds 1–4 of face = 2¼ inches

Pattern Note

Using directions and colors indicated, follow instructions for Basic Friend on page 1.

Kitty Friend

Face

Rnds 1–12: With lemon.

Rnds 13 & 14: With gold.

Rnds 15 & 16: With lemon.

Rnd 17: With gold.

Back of Head

Rnds 1–4: With lemon.

Rnds 5–16: Work [2 rnds with gold, 2 rnds with lemon] 3 times.

Rnd 17: With gold.

Body

Rows 1–5: Work [1 row with lemon, 1 row with gold] 2 times, then 1 row with lemon.

First Arm

Row 1: With gold.

Row 2: With lemon.

Rows 3 & 4: With soft white.

Continue Body

Rows 6–9: Work [1 row with gold, 1 row with lemon] 2 times.

First Leg

Rows 1–4: Work [1 row with gold, 1 row with lemon] 2 times.

Rows 5 & 6: With soft white.

2nd Leg

Rows 1–4: Work [1 row with gold, 1 row with lemon] 2 times.

Rows 5 & 6: With soft white.

2nd Arm

Row 1: With gold.

Row 2: With lemon.

Rows 3 & 4: With soft white.

Tummy

Rnds 1–6: With soft white.

Ear

Make 2.

Row 1 (RS): With gold, ch 6, dc in 4th ch from hook, hdc in next ch, (2 sc, ch 2, 2 sc) in last ch. Now working along opposite side of beg ch, hdc in next ch, dc in each of last 2 chs. Fasten off gold, turn. *(2 dc, 1 hdc, 2 sc, 1 ch-2 sp, 2 sc, 1 hdc, 2 dc)*

Row 2 (RS): Join soft white in first dc, ch 1, sc in same st, sc in next st, 2 sc in next st, sc in next 2 sts, (sc, ch 2, sc) in ch-2 sp, sc in next 2 sts, 2 sc in next st, sc in last 2 sts. Fasten off soft white, turn. *(7 sc, 1 ch-2 sp, 7 sc)*

Row 3: Join lemon in first sc, ch 1, sc in same st, sc in next 3 sts, 2 sc in next st, sc in next 2 sts, (sc, ch 2, sc) in ch-2 sp, sc in next 2 sts, 2 sc in next st, sc in last 4 sts. Fasten off. *(9 sc, 1 ch-2 sp, 9 sc)*

Tail

Row 1: With soft white, ch 2, 2 sc in 2nd ch from hook, turn. *(2 sc)*

Row 2: Ch 1, sc in same st, sc in next st. Fasten off soft white, turn. *(2 sc)*

Row 3: Join lemon in first sc, ch 1, sc in same st, sc in next st, turn.

Row 4: Ch 1, sc in same st, sc in next st. Fasten off lemon, turn.

Rows 5–14: Alternating 2 rows with gold and 2 rows with lemon, ch 1, sc in same st, sc in next st, turn. At end of row 14, fasten off. *(2 sc)*

Finishing

See Kitty diagram for ear and facial feature placement. Assemble as for Basic Friend. ●

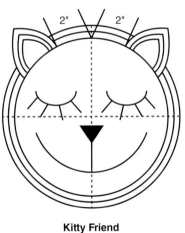

Kitty Friend
Diagram

Lamb Friend

Skill Level

 EASY

Finished Measurement

18 inches tall

Materials

- Red Heart Super Saver medium (worsted) weight acrylic yarn (7 oz/364 yds/198g per skein):
  - 1 skein each #316 soft white and #336 warm brown
  - 10 yds #235 lemon
  - 4 yds #312 black
- Size H/8/5mm crochet hook or size needed to obtain gauge
- 10-inch round pillow or fiberfill
- Stitch markers: 8
- Tapestry needle

Gauge

Rnds 1–4 of face = 2¼ inches

Pattern Note

Using directions and colors indicated, follow instructions for Basic Friend on page 1.

Lamb Friend

Face

Rnds 1–12: With warm brown.

Rnds 13–17: With soft white.

Back of Head

Rnds 1–17: With soft white.

Body

Rows 1–5: With soft white.

First Arm

Rows 1 & 2: With soft white.

Rows 3 & 4: With warm brown.

Continue Body

Rows 6–9: With soft white.

First Leg

Rows 1–4: With soft white.

Rows 5 & 6: With warm brown.

2nd Leg

Rows 1–4: With soft white.

Rows 5 & 6: With warm brown.

2nd Arm

Rows 1 & 2: With soft white.

Rows 3 & 4: With warm brown.

Tummy

Rnds 1–6: With warm brown.

Ear

Make 2.

Row 1 (RS): With warm brown, ch 13, dc in 4th ch from hook, dc in next 8 chs, 7 dc in last ch. Now working along opposite side of beg ch, dc in next 10 chs, turn. *(27 dc)*

Row 2: Ch 1, sc in same st, sc in next 3 sts, hdc in next 3 sts, dc in next 2 sts, (2 dc in next st, dc in next st) 5 times, dc in next st, hdc in next 3 sts, sc in last 4 sts. Fasten off. *(4 sc, 3 hdc, 18 dc, 3 hdc, 4 sc)*

Tail

Row 1: With soft white, ch 2, 3 sc in 2nd ch from hook, turn. *(3 sc)*

Row 2: Ch 1, 2 sc in same st, sc in next st, 2 sc in last st, turn. *(5 sc)*

Rows 3–5: Ch 1, sc in same st, sc in each st across, turn. *(5 sc)*

Row 6: Ch 1, **sc dec** *(see Stitch Guide)* over first 2 sts, sc in next st, sc dec over last 2 sts, turn. *(3 sc)*

Row 7: Ch 1, sc in same st, sc in each st across. Fasten off. *(3 sc)*

Bow

All rows: With lemon.

Finishing

See Lamb diagram for ear and facial feature placement. Assemble as for Basic Friend. ●

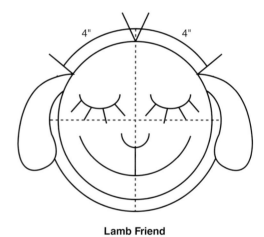

Lamb Friend
Diagram

Lion Friend

Skill Level

 ■■□□ EASY

Finished Measurement

18 inches tall

Materials

- Red Heart Super Saver medium (worsted) weight acrylic yarn (7 oz/364 yds/198g per skein):
    1 skein each #320 cornmeal, #316 soft white and #360 cafe latte
    5 yds #312 black
- Size H/8/5mm crochet hook or size needed to obtain gauge
- 10-inch round pillow or fiberfill
- Stitch markers: 8
- Tapestry needle

Gauge

Rnds 1–4 of face = 2¼ inches

Pattern Notes

Using directions and colors indicated, follow instructions for Basic Friend on page 1.

Chain-2 at beginning of row does not count as first stitch unless otherwise stated.

Lion Friend

Face

Rnds 1–12: With cornmeal, do not fasten off at end of rnd 12.

Rnds 13 & 14: With cornmeal. Fasten off at end of rnd 14.

Rnd 15: Join cafe latte in **back lp** *(see Stitch Guide)* of first st, working back lps only for this rnd.

Rnds 16 & 17: With cafe latte.

Mane

Working in **front lps** *(see Stitch Guide)* of rnd 15, join cafe latte in any st, (ch 15, sl st in next st) around, ending with ch 15, sl st in first st. Fasten off. *(74 ch-15 lps)*

Back of Head

Rnds 1–17: With cafe latte.

Body

Rows 1–5: With cornmeal.

First Arm

Rows 1 & 2: With cornmeal.

Rows 3 & 4: With soft white.

Continue Body

Rows 6–9: With cornmeal.

First Leg

Rows 1–4: With cornmeal.

Rows 5 & 6: With soft white.

2nd Leg

Rows 1–4: With cornmeal.

Rows 5 & 6: With soft white.

2nd Arm

Rows 1 & 2: With cornmeal.

Rows 3 & 4: With soft white.

Tummy

Rnds 1–6: With soft white.

Ear

Make 2.

Row 1: With cafe latte, ch 6, dc in 4th ch from hook, hdc in next ch, 5 sc in last ch. Now working along opposite side of beg ch, hdc in next ch, dc in each of last 2 chs. Fasten off cafe latte, turn. *(2 dc, 1 hdc, 5 sc, 1 hdc, 2 dc)*

Row 2 (RS): Join soft white in first dc, ch 1, sc in same st, sc in next 2 sts, 2 sc in next st, sc in next 3 sts, 2 sc in next st, sc in last 3 sts. Fasten off soft white, turn. *(13 sc)*

Row 3: Join cornmeal in first sc, ch 1, sc in same st, (sc in next 3 sts, 2 sc in next st) 2 times, sc in last 4 sts. Fasten off. *(15 sc)*

Tail

Row 1: With cornmeal, ch 3, sc in 2nd ch from hook, sc in next ch, turn. *(2 sc)*

Rows 2–12: Ch 1, sc in same st, sc in next st, turn. At end of row 12, fasten off, turn. *(2 sc)*

Row 13: Join cafe latte in first st, ch 8, sl st in same st, ch 12, sl st in next st, ch 8, sl st in same st. Fasten off. *(ch-8 lp, ch-12 lp, ch-8 lp)*

Finishing

See Lion diagram for ear and facial feature placement. Assemble as for Basic Friend. ●

Lion Friend
Diagram

Piggy Friend

Skill Level
 EASY

Finished Measurement
18 inches tall

Materials
- Red Heart Super Saver medium (worsted) weight acrylic yarn (7 oz/364 yds/198g per skein):

  - 1 skein each #724 baby pink and #373 petal pink
  - 10 yds each #312 black and #885 Delft blue
- Size H/8/5mm crochet hook or size needed to obtain gauge
- 10-inch round pillow or fiberfill
- Stitch markers: 8
- Tapestry needle

Gauge
Rnds 1–4 of face = 2¼ inches

Pattern Note
Using directions and colors indicated, follow instructions for Basic Friend on page 1.

Piggy Friend

Face
Rnds 1–12: With baby pink.

Rnds 13–17: With petal pink.

Back of Head
Rnds 1–17: With petal pink.

Body
Rows 1–5: With petal pink.

First Arm
Rows 1 & 2: With petal pink.

Rows 3 & 4: With black.

Continue Body
Rows 6–9: With petal pink.

First Leg
Rows 1–4: With petal pink.

Rows 5 & 6: With black.

2nd Leg
Rows 1–4: With petal pink.

Rows 5 & 6: With black.

2nd Arm
Rows 1 & 2: With petal pink.

Rows 3 & 4: With black.

Tummy
Rnds 1–6: With baby pink.

Ear
Make 2.

Row 1 (RS): With baby pink, ch 7, dc in 4th ch from hook, dc in next ch, hdc in next ch, (2 sc, ch 2, 2 sc) in last ch. Now working along opposite side of beg ch, hdc in next ch, dc in last 3 chs, turn. *(3 dc, 1 hdc, 2 sc, 1 ch-2 sp, 2 sc, 1 hdc, 3 dc)*

Row 2 (RS): Ch 1, sc in same st, hdc in next st, 2 dc in next st, hdc in next 2 sts, sc in next st, (sc, ch 2, sc) in ch-2 sp, sc in next st, hdc in next 2 sts, 2 dc in next st, hdc in next st, sc in last st, turn. *(1 sc, 1 hdc, 2 dc, 2 hdc, 2 sc, 1 ch-2 sp, 2 sc, 2 hdc, 2 dc, 1 hdc, 1 sc)*

Row 3: Ch 1, sc in same st, hdc in next st, (2 dc in next st) 2 times, hdc in next 2 sts, sc in next 2 sts, (sc, ch 2, sc) in ch-2 sp, sc in next 2 sts, hdc in next 2 sts, (2 dc in next st) 2 times, hdc in next st, sc in last st. Fasten off baby pink, turn. *(1 sc, 1 hdc, 4 dc, 2 hdc, 3 sc, 1 ch-2 sp, 3 sc, 2 hdc, 4 dc, 1 hdc, 1 sc)*

Row 4: Join petal pink in first st, ch 1, sc in same st, sc in next st, *(2 sc in next st, sc in next 2 sts) 2 times*, sc in next 3 sts, (sc, ch 2, sc) in ch-2 sp, sc in next 5 sts, rep between *. Fasten off. *(14 sc, 1 ch-2 sp, 14 sc)*

Tail
With petal pink, ch 10, 2 sc in 2nd ch from hook, 2 sc in each ch across. Fasten off. *(18 sc)*

Bow
All rows: With Delft blue.

Finishing
See Piggy diagram for ear and facial feature placement. Assemble as for Basic Friend. ●

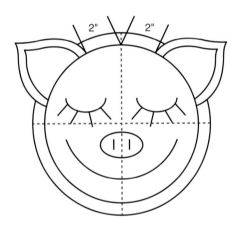

Piggy Friend
Diagram

Tiger Friend

Skill Level

 EASY

Finished Measurement

18 inches tall

Materials

- Red Heart Super Saver medium (worsted) weight acrylic yarn (7 oz/364 yds/198g per skein): 1 skein each #316 soft white, #312 black and #254 pumpkin
- Size H/8/5mm crochet hook or size needed to obtain gauge
- 10-inch round pillow or fiberfill
- Stitch markers: 8
- Tapestry needle

Gauge

Rnds 1–4 of face = 2¼ inches

Pattern Note

Using directions and colors indicated, follow instructions for Basic Friend on page 1.

Tiger Friend

Face

Rnds 1–12: With pumpkin.

Rnds 13 & 14: With black.

Rnds 15–17: With soft white.

Back of Head

Rnds 1–4: With pumpkin.

Rnds 5–14: Work 2 rnds with black, [2 rnds with pumpkin, 2 rnds with black] 2 times.

Rnds 15–17: With pumpkin.

Body

Rows 1–5: Work [1 row with pumpkin, 1 row with black] 2 times, then 1 row with pumpkin.

First Arm

Row 1: With black.

Row 2: With pumpkin.

Rows 3 & 4: With soft white.

Continue Body

Rows 6–9: Work [1 row with black, 1 row with pumpkin] 2 times.

First Leg

Rows 1–4: Work [1 row with black, 1 row with pumpkin] 2 times.

Rows 5 & 6: With soft white.

2nd Leg

Rows 1–4: Work [1 row with black, 1 row with pumpkin] 2 times.

Rows 5 & 6: With soft white.

2nd Arm

Row 1: With black.

Row 2: With pumpkin.

Rows 3 & 4: With soft white.

Tummy

Rnds 1–6: With soft white.

Ear

Make 2.

Row 1: With black, ch 6, dc in 4th ch from hook, hdc in next ch, 5 sc in last ch. Now working along opposite side of beg ch, hdc in next ch, dc in each of last 2 chs. Fasten off black, turn. *(2 dc, 1 hdc, 5 sc, 1 hdc, 2 dc)*

Row 2 (RS): Join soft white in first dc, ch 1, sc in same st, sc in next 2 sts, 2 sc in next st, sc in next 3 sts, 2 sc in next st, sc in last 3 sts. Fasten off soft white, turn. *(13 sc)*

Row 3: Join pumpkin in first sc, ch 1, sc in same st, (sc in next 3 sts, 2 sc in next st) 2 times, sc in last 4 sts. Fasten off. *(15 sc)*

Tail

Row 1: With black, ch 2, 2 sc in 2nd ch from hook, turn. *(2 sc)*

Row 2: Ch 1, sc in same st, sc in next st. Fasten off black, turn. *(2 sc)*

Row 3: Join soft white in first sc, ch 1, sc in same st, sc in next st, turn.

Row 4: Ch 1, sc in same st, sc in next st. Fasten off soft white, turn.

Rows 5–14: Alternating 2 rows black and 2 rows soft white, ch 1, sc in same st, sc in next st, turn. At end of row 14, fasten off. *(2 sc)*

Finishing

See Tiger diagram for ear and facial feature placement. Assemble as for Basic Friend. ●

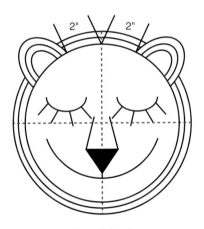

Tiger Friend
Diagram

Metric Conversion Charts

METRIC CONVERSIONS

yards	x	.9144	=	meters (m)
yards	x	91.44	=	centimeters (cm)
inches	x	2.54	=	centimeters (cm)
inches	x	25.40	=	millimeters (mm)
inches	x	.0254	=	meters (m)

centimeters	x	.3937	=	inches
meters	x	1.0936	=	yards

INCHES INTO MILLIMETERS & CENTIMETERS (Rounded off slightly)

inches	mm	cm	inches	cm	inches	cm	inches	cm
1/8	3	0.3	5	12.5	21	53.5	38	96.5
1/4	6	0.6	5 1/2	14	22	56	39	99
3/8	10	1	6	15	23	58.5	40	101.5
1/2	13	1.3	7	18	24	61	41	104
5/8	15	1.5	8	20.5	25	63.5	42	106.5
3/4	20	2	9	23	26	66	43	109
7/8	22	2.2	10	25.5	27	68.5	44	112
1	25	2.5	11	28	28	71	45	114.5
1 1/4	32	3.2	12	30.5	29	73.5	46	117
1 1/2	38	3.8	13	33	30	76	47	119.5
1 3/4	45	4.5	14	35.5	31	79	48	122
2	50	5	15	38	32	81.5	49	124.5
2 1/2	65	6.5	16	40.5	33	84	50	127
3	75	7.5	17	43	34	86.5		
3 1/2	90	9	18	46	35	89		
4	100	10	19	48.5	36	91.5		
4 1/2	115	11.5	20	51	37	94		

KNITTING NEEDLES CONVERSION CHART

Canada/U.S.	0	1	2	3	4	5	6	7	8	9	10	10½	11	13	15
Metric (mm)	2	2¼	2¾	3¼	3½	3¾	4	4½	5	5½	6	6½	8	9	10

CROCHET HOOKS CONVERSION CHART

Canada/U.S.	1/B	2/C	3/D	4/E	5/F	6/G	7	8/H	9/I	10/J	10½/K	N
Metric (mm)	2.25	2.75	3.25	3.5	3.75	4	4.5	5	5.5	6	6.5	9.0

STITCH GUIDE

 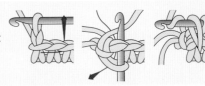

STITCH ABBREVIATIONS

beg	begin/begins/beginning
bpdc	back post double crochet
bpsc	back post single crochet
bptr	back post treble crochet
CC	contrasting color
ch(s)	chain(s)
ch-	refers to chain or space previously made (i.e., ch-1 space)
ch sp(s)	chain space(s)
cl(s)	cluster(s)
cm	centimeter(s)
dc	double crochet (singular/plural)
dc dec	double crochet 2 or more stitches together, as indicated
dec	decrease/decreases/decreasing
dtr	double treble crochet
ext	extended
fpdc	front post double crochet
fpsc	front post single crochet
fptr	front post treble crochet
g	gram(s)
hdc	half double crochet
hdc dec	half double crochet 2 or more stitches together, as indicated
inc	increase/increases/increasing
lp(s)	loop(s)
MC	main color
mm	millimeter(s)
oz	ounce(s)
pc	popcorn(s)
rem	remain/remains/remaining
rep(s)	repeat(s)
rnd(s)	round(s)
RS	right side
sc	single crochet (singular/plural)
sc dec	single crochet 2 or more stitches together, as indicated
sk	skip/skipped/skipping
sl st(s)	slip stitch(es)
sp(s)	space(s)/spaced
st(s)	stitch(es)
tog	together
tr	treble crochet
trtr	triple treble
WS	wrong side
yd(s)	yard(s)
yo	yarn over

YARN CONVERSION

OUNCES TO GRAMS	GRAMS TO OUNCES
1 .... 28.4	25 .... ⅞
2 .... 56.7	40 .... 1⅔
3 .... 85.0	50 .... 1¾
4 .... 113.4	100 .... 3½

UNITED STATES		UNITED KINGDOM
sl st (slip stitch)	=	sc (single crochet)
sc (single crochet)	=	dc (double crochet)
hdc (half double crochet)	=	htr (half treble crochet)
dc (double crochet)	=	tr (treble crochet)
tr (treble crochet)	=	dtr (double treble crochet)
dtr (double treble crochet)	=	ttr (triple treble crochet)
skip	=	miss

Single crochet decrease (sc dec): (Insert hook, yo, draw lp through) in each of the sts indicated, yo, draw through all lps on hook.

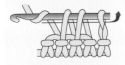

Example of 2-sc dec

Half double crochet decrease (hdc dec): (Yo, insert hook, yo, draw lp through) in each of the sts indicated, yo, draw through all lps on hook.

Example of 2-hdc dec

Reverse single crochet (reverse sc): Ch 1, sk first st, working from left to right, insert hook in next st from front to back, draw up lp on hook, yo and draw through both lps on hook.

Chain (ch): Yo, pull through lp on hook.

Single crochet (sc): Insert hook in st, yo, pull through st, yo, pull through both lps on hook.

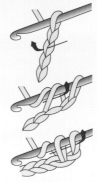

Double crochet (dc): Yo, insert hook in st, yo, pull through st, [yo, pull through 2 lps] twice.

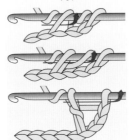

Front loop (front lp) Back loop (back lp)

Front Loop   Back Loop

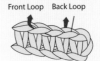

Front post stitch (fp): Back post stitch (bp): When working post st, insert hook from right to left around post of st on previous row.

Back   Front

Post of Stitch

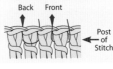

Half double crochet (hdc): Yo, insert hook in st, yo, pull through st, yo, pull through all 3 lps on hook.

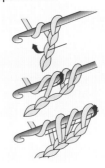

Double treble crochet (dtr): Yo 3 times, insert hook in st, yo, pull through st, [yo, pull through 2 lps] 4 times.

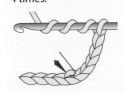

Slip stitch (sl st): Insert hook in st, pull through both lps on hook.

Chain color change (ch color change) Yo with new color, draw through last lp on hook.

Double crochet color change (dc color change) Drop first color, yo with new color, draw through last 2 lps of st.

Treble crochet (tr): Yo twice, insert hook in st, yo, pull through st, [yo, pull through 2 lps] 3 times.

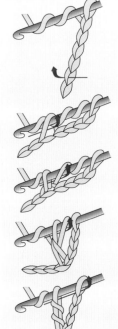

Double crochet decrease (dc dec): (Yo, insert hook, yo, draw lp through, yo, draw through 2 lps on hook) in each of the sts indicated, yo, draw through all lps on hook.

Example of 2-dc dec

Treble crochet decrease (tr dec): Holding back last lp of each st, tr in each of the sts indicated, yo, pull through all lps on hook.

Example of 2-tr dec

Annie's® *My Sleepy-Time Friends Crochet Pillows* is published by Annie's, 306 East Parr Road, Berne, IN 46711. Printed in USA. Copyright © 2018 Annie's. All rights reserved. This publication may not be reproduced in part or in whole without written permission from the publisher.

RETAIL STORES: If you would like to carry this publication or any other Annie's publication, visit AnniesWSL.com.

Every effort has been made to ensure that the instructions in this publication are complete and accurate. We cannot, however, take responsibility for human error, typographical mistakes or variations in individual work. Please visit AnniesCustomerService.com to check for pattern updates.

ISBN: 978-1-59012-923-4

1 2 3 4 5 6 7 8 9